GER

GALLERY COLLECTION

RIC STEININGER GALLERY

LAHAINA ⓒ CAIRNS ⓒ LAS VEGAS

Ric Steininger Gallery

Cairns

63 Abbott Street (cnr Spence), Cairns City
Post: PO Box 12269D, Cairns Qld 4870, Australia
Phone: 011-61-7-40521-533, Fax: 011-61-7-40313-688
Email: cairns@steininger.com.au

Hawaii Gallery

815 Front Street, Lahaina Town, Maui
Post: Box 11737, Lahaina, HI 96761
Phone: (808) 667-7008, Fax: (808) 667-6801, Toll Free: (866) 826-6284
Email: lahaina@steininger.com.au

Las Vegas Showroom

The Signature at MGM Grand
125 East Harmon Avenue Suite 1414, Las Vegas, NV 89109
Phone: (702) 797-6000 Ext. 1414

Web: www.steininger.com.au

Photography, text and design by Ric Steininger
Text edited by Salli-Anne Hart

Published in Cairns Australia, August 2007

Copyright © Ric J. Steininger Publications Pty Ltd 1992 - 2007

ISBN 0-9581633-5-4   All rights reserved

Printed in China by Everbest Printing Company Ltd

INTRODUCTION

Welcome to the limited edition *Ric Steininger Gallery Collection*, a journey through the camera lens into the vivid world of photographic art.

I take great delight in that my work gives me an excuse to get out and explore some of the most beautiful and dramatic places in the world. I love the challenge of dealing with all the natural elements and the chance moments that arise that allow me to capture what nature has presented. What is truly rewarding to me is not only discovering the scene in the first place; it's being there to capture it when it all happens.

I felt earlier on with my work that I should study traditional arts, to learn to paint. In reality it is really difficult to find scenes and photograph them with the drama and the lighting that I envision. This is the one thing with my work — it demands that I be there, the location has to exist; the conditions, the lighting, the mood, all have to be right. But to me, in the end, that is half the fun. I love this art form, this medium, the challenge of deeply involving myself with natural world and capturing it on film. That chance moment of drama, life and inspiration. My work starts in my mind as an idea, and then I have to search for it and discover it, experience it and be a part of it.

When selecting each piece for this collection, I endeavored to showcase the essence of my passion for pure photographic art. I am deeply committed to portraying natural beauty as it appears to the naked eye — I do not employ the use of color filters. The rich colors and awesome beauty in each image are the result of finding just the right position, and waiting for the ideal natural light.

In this collection, beneath most of the photographs, there is a brief record of the adventure behind the art. Whether captured in North America, Australia, or Japan, each photograph is the result of a great quest. I have dangled precariously out of helicopters, braved the heat and danger of molten lava flows, carried my equipment over kilometers of rugged terrain, and spent many a sleepless night in the wilderness and pouring rain, all to capture on film the vision set before me in my mind's eye.

The limited edition photographs in this collection are best viewed as they are intended: as framed photographic art pieces. I welcome you to visit one of my galleries.

Enjoy!

4   Bamboo

I spent five days photographing bamboo across a number of great sites, and was inspired by the spectrum of vivid green and tan tones. One of the sites had a lovely creek, but as I was shooting the wind kept picking up, causing the bamboo to sway. The long exposures meant that it was impossible to capture a crisp, clear image at that site. Even so, I persisted and found a site with adequate stillness and an incredible play of light, captured above.

Camera: Tomiyama, lens Nikkor SW90, **Film:** Fuji Velvia 100F, **Shutter speed:** 15 seconds, **Filters:** none, **Cropping:** none, **Time/Conditions:** mid-afternoon, partially cloudy

Limited Edition release: 750 only worldwide, **Exclusivity:** open

There is a gentle peace in spending time in these places: quietude all around except for sounds of flowing water and the light rustle of wind through the greenery above.

Camera: Tomiyama, lens Nikkor SW90, **Film:** Fuji Velvia 100ASA, **Shutter speed:** 8 seconds, **Filters:** none, **Cropping:** none, **Time/Conditions:** afternoon, raining
Limited Edition release: 750 only worldwide, **Exclusivity:** open

When I look at this photograph, I have a sense of being on top of the world, as if I am dwelling in the heavens. I love the glory of all the light and color as it moves gently in and amongst the clouds.

Camera: Tomiyama, lens Nikkor SW90, **Film:** Fuji Velvia 100F, **Shutter speed:** 1 second, **Filters:** none, **Cropping:** 20%, **Time/Conditions:** sunrise
Limited Edition release: 750 only worldwide, **Exclusivity:** open

Brilliant dawn light dancing across the clouds, captured at 10,000 feet above sea level.

Camera: Tomiyama, lens Nikkor SW90, **Film:** Fuji Velvia 100F, **Shutter speed:** 15 second, **Filters:** none, **Cropping:** 20%, **Time/Conditions:** 30 min. before sunrise
Limited Edition release: 750 only worldwide, **Exclusivity:** open

Kilauea volcano, Hawaii

I had a challenging and fun time shooting this volcano in Hawaii. I spent a night hiking around the lava fields, searching for my shot. As I hiked across Lava tubes, I looked down at the glowing, molten flow thinking to myself, "What am I doing? This is crazy!" It took four hours to get to where I wanted to shoot and I set up. Then it rained. It rained and rained. The sun sank below the horizon and it continued to rain - and no photograph. I started to hike back in the dark, pummeled by the wind and torrential rain, across the active lava field. The rain on the hot lava produced so much steam that I couldn't even see my feet at times.

Arriving at the half way point, the rain eased. I sat down to dry myself off and became warmer from the heat of the lava. I photographed the surface lava for the next three hours. As morning neared, I headed towards the ocean to shoot the lava entering into sea at sunrise.

Camera: Linhoff Technorama, 180mm lens,   **Film:** Fuji Velvia 100F,   **Shutter speed:** 4 seconds,   **Cropping:** none,   **Time/Conditions:** sunrise

Limited Edition release: 750 only worldwide,   **Exclusivity:** open

13

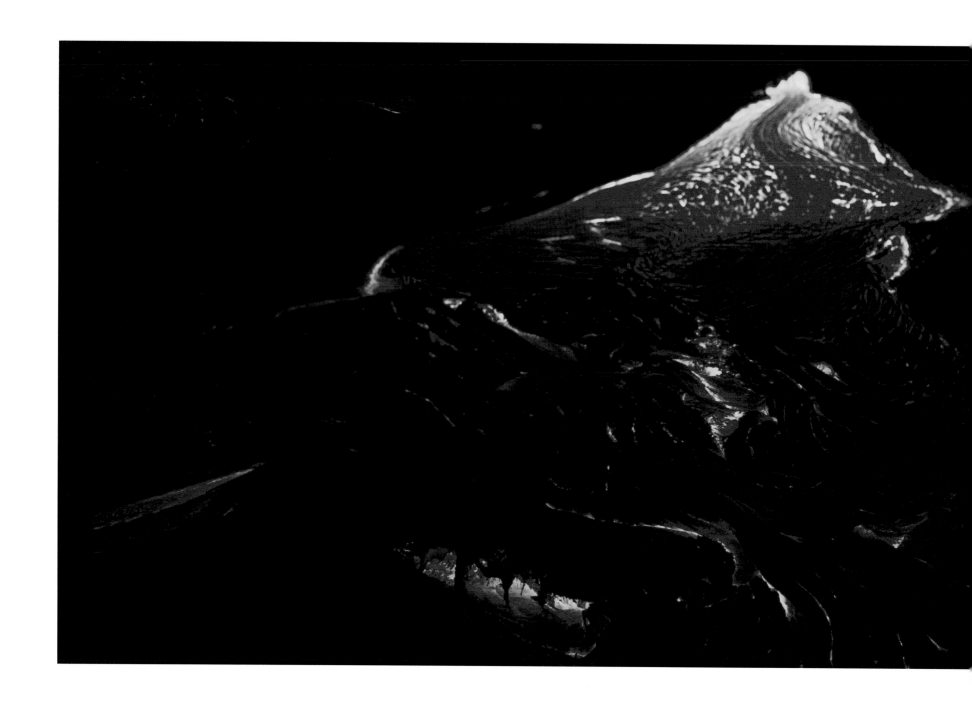

Madame Pele

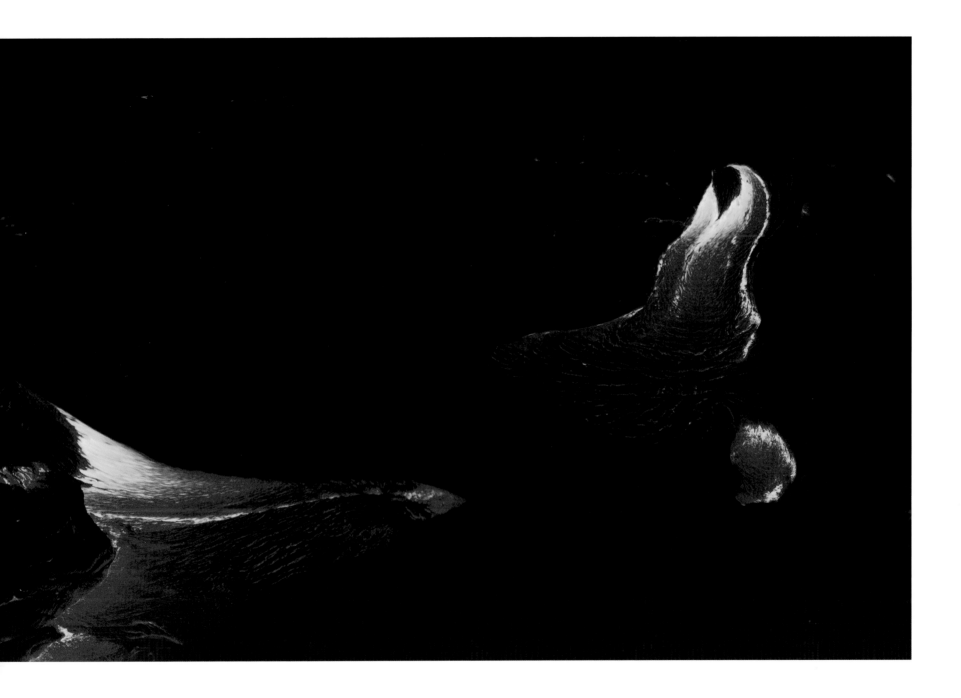

Kilauea volcano, Hawaii

I relish the adventure and challenge of shots like this one. In such close proximity, the heat of the lava was intense. At one point, my tripod became too hot to pick up; I worried that the lens of my camera would crack with the heat. Most of the time the lava was slow moving, but in this particular scene, the lava moved unexpectedly quickly, and I had to get out of the way.

I worked most of the night. At one time I lay down on the lava rock with a towel under my head. I gazed at the full moon and dozed off for twenty minutes or so.

Camera: Linhoff Technorama, 180mm lens,   **Film:** Fuji Velvia 100F,   **Shutter speed:** 4 seconds,   **Cropping:** none,   **Time/Conditions:** 12-3am, intermittent rain

Limited Edition release: 750 only worldwide,   **Exclusivity:** open

Maui, Hawaii

I love Maui, it has become my second home. From the house where I live it is possible to see the sun as it sets over the island of Lanai. There is such a variety of colors; each sunset is different. I set myself up ready every day to make the dash to my chosen vantage point. This particular day was spectacular.

From Maui you can easily see whales as they travel back to Alaska. You can see them breaching and their water spraying up high when they come up for air - an awesome sight.

Camera: Tomiyama, lens Nikkor SW90, **Film:** Fuji Velvia 100F, **Shutter speed:** 1/15 second, **Filters:** none, **Cropping:** none, **Time/Conditions:** sunset
Limited Edition release: 750 only worldwide, **Exclusivity:** open

Maui, Hawaii

Captured 20 minutes after sunset, the last glow of the sun hit the clouds up high, lighting them in a rich pink hue.

Camera: Tomiyama, lens Nikkor SW90, **Film:** Fuji Velvia 100F, **Shutter speed:** 1/4 second, **Filters:** none, **Cropping:** none, **Time/Conditions:** sunset
Limited Edition release: 750 only worldwide, **Exclusivity:** open

Colorful eucalypt trees (gums), Hawaii

For us Australians ('Aussies') it is incredible to find gum trees in Hawaii, especially such a beautiful variety. I have never seen such a colorful display before. The richness of the reds, yellows and olive greens is amazing. The variation in each of these trees is fantastic! Appropriately referred to as 'Rainbow Eucalyptus', as I researched these trees I found that they are not native to Australia, but are native to a small island in the Philippines.

Camera: Tomiyama, lens Nikkor SW90, **Film:** Fuji Velvia 100F, **Shutter speed:** 15 seconds, **Filters:** polarized, **Cropping:** none, **Time/Conditions:** mid-afternoon, partially cloudy
Limited Edition release: 750 only worldwide, **Exclusivity:** open

A Banyan tree set in the mountains of Hawaii.

The mountains in Hawaii are typically covered in cloud. The moss on these rocks is so rich – I can only conclude that the area is shaded by the mountains; the mist and moisture lingering around unspoiled. Close to here, on this trail, the cliffs climb high and steep. The views of the dramatic coastline are very impressive and powerful. This is a tranquil, peaceful location, a mystical, other-worldly place where I could spend endless time.

Camera: Tomiyama, lens Nikkor SW90,　**Film:** Fuji Velvia 100F,　**Shutter speed:** 30 seconds,　**Filters:** none,　**Cropping:** none,　**Time/Conditions:** mid-day

Limited Edition release: 750 only worldwide,　**Exclusivity:** open

Molokai, Hawaii

Molokai, Hawaii, is an amazing place, untouched. In this area, local Hawaiians still use this ancient pond to farm fish. This side of the island is protected from the weather by the island of Maui, as well as a coral shelf that extends into the ocean. The wall around this pond was constructed eight-hundred years ago and still remains today. There are approximately 60 man-made ponds, however only a few are still used for their original purpose: fish farming.

Camera: Tomiyama, lens Nikkor SW90,   **Film:** Fuji Velvia 100F,   **Shutter speed:** 1/4 second,   **Filters:** polarized,   **Cropping:** none,   **Time/Conditions:** early morning, calm
Limited Edition release: 750 only worldwide,   **Exclusivity:** open

Molokai, Hawaii

Morning tranquility. Photographed near some fishing ponds, this area is untouched. When the trade winds aren't blowing, the waters on this side of the island become incredibly tranquil. Going right out to the open ocean, the waters are calm; you can just see where the coral shelf ends near the horizon.

Camera: Tomiyama, lens Nikkor SW90, **Film:** Fuji Velvia 100F, **Shutter speed:** 1/8 seconds, **Filters:** polarized, **Cropping:** none, **Time/Conditions:** early morning, calm
Limited Edition release: 750 only worldwide, **Exclusivity:** open

Molokai, Hawaii
This is a most grand and powerful sight to see. Molokai has the highest sea cliffs in the world, with elegant waterfalls gracefully falling into the sea.

Camera: Tomiyama, lens Nikkor SW90, **Film:** Fuji Velvia 100F, **Shutter speed:** 1/30 second, **Filters:** polarized, **Cropping:** none, **Time/Conditions:** mid-morning
Limited Edition release: 750 only worldwide, **Exclusivity:** open

Molokai, Hawaii

Camera: Tomiyama, lens Nikkor SW90, **Film:** Fuji Velvia 100F, **Shutter speed:** 1/4 second, **Filters:** none, **Cropping:** none, **Time/Conditions:** sunset
Limited Edition release: 750 only worldwide, **Exclusivity:** open

Molokai, Hawaii

Camera: Tomiyama, lens Nikkor SW90, **Film:** Fuji 100ASA, **Shutter speed:** 1 second,
Filters: none, **Cropping:** none, **Time/Conditions:** early morning
Limited Edition release: 750 only worldwide, **Exclusivity:** open

Camera: Tomiyama, lens Nikkor SW90,   Film: Fuji Velvia 100F,   Shutter speed: 1 second,
Filters: none,   Cropping: 20%,   Time/Conditions: sunrise
Limited Edition release: 750 only worldwide,   Exclusivity: open

Whitehaven Beach, Whitsunday Islands, Australia

Whitehaven Beach is famous for its brilliant white sands. It is one of the most beautiful beaches in the world. Totally untouched, no buildings, barely anyone to be seen, except a stray yacht passing by. The aqua colored waters are so inviting.

Camera: Linhoff Technorama, Super Angulon 72 mm lens,   **Film:** Fuji Velvia 100F,   **Shutter speed:** 1/30 second,   **Filters:** polarized,   **Cropping:** none,   **Time/Conditions:** late morning
Limited Edition release: 750 only worldwide,   **Exclusivity:** open

The Great Barrier Reef Australia.

Whitehaven beach is commonly referred to as the most beautiful beach in the world. The brilliant, pure white sand covers the full length of the beach, the alluring turquoise water and various islands in the distance. It is a sailor's dream spot to anchor and touches the heart of everyone who visits.

Flying in on a small Bell helicopter with floats, I landed here looking for a sand bar to shoot. I set up these deck chairs and had to keep moving them as the tide came in.

Camera: Tomiyama, lens Nikkor SW90,   **Film:** Fuji 100ASA,   **Shutter speed:** 1/125 second,   **Filters:** polarized,   **Cropping:** none,   **Time/Conditions:** mid-day
Limited Edition release: 360 only worldwide,   **Exclusivity:** open

I spent four hours flying around Hardy Reef in the Whitsundays, choosing this reef because of the dramatic channel that separates the two reefs. The channel is 600 feet (200 meters) wide and 360 feet (120 meters) deep, from the shallow coral to the ocean bed. I spent the better part of a day flying in a plane at around 5000 feet. I was tightly strapped in with the door off, confronting the noise, engine fumes, and freezing cold. It was simultaneously nauseating and exhilarating. 'Great Reef' was captured at around 3000 feet.

On the left-hand-side of the photograph, three fingers of coral lead up to the edge of the reef; on the right, the sunlight sparkles on the water. In the centre, a boat is anchored and snorkelers swim on the reef wall.

Camera: Tomiyama, lens Nikkor SW90,   **Film:** Fuji 100ASA,   **Shutter speed:** 1/125 second,   **Filters:** polarized,   **Cropping:** none,   **Time/Conditions:** mid-day

Limited Edition release: 360 only worldwide,   **Exclusivity:** open

Camera: Tomiyama, lens Nikkor SW90,   Film: Fuji 100ASA,   Shutter speed: 1/125 second,   Filters: polarized,   Cropping: none,   Time/Conditions: mid-afternoon
Limited Edition release: 360 only worldwide,   Exclusivity: open

The Great Barrier Reef Australia.

A view looking back to my home town of Cairns, with Green Island in the foreground.

Coral islands like these are simply paradise for all who visit. This island boasts shady palm trees, white sand beaches and great snorkeling in the aqua colored waters amongst a variety of tropical coral fish and turtles.

Camera: Tomiyama, lens Nikkor SW90,   **Film:** Fuji Velvia 100F,   **Shutter speed:** 1/125 second,   **Filters:** polarized,   **Cropping:** none,   **Time/Conditions:** mid-afternoon

Limited Edition release: 360 only worldwide,   **Exclusivity:** open

The Great Barrier Reef, Australia.

An unbelievable sight. The natural formation of reef known as Heart Reef seems closer to fantasy than reality. Heart Reef is quite small and is situated in the midst of a large enclosed reef.

Camera: Tomiyama, lens Nikkor SW90, **Film:** Fuji 100ASA, **Shutter speed:** 1/125 second, **Filters:** polarized, **Cropping:** none, **Time/Conditions:** mid-day
Limited Edition release: 360 only worldwide, **Exclusivity:** open

Little Upolu

A sand cay in the Great Barrier Reef, Australia.

First, many thanks must go to my wife Michiko who sat patiently for over 13 hours whilst I photographed "Little Upolu". I worked on the concept of white sand and blue reef waters with a human touch for a few months. This scene required a lot of planning, research, sketching and visualization before I photographed it. After considering the use of a helicopter, a plane and the (rather dangerous) possibility of climbing the sail mast of a yacht, I decided that a game fishing boat with a 45 foot high tower offered the greatest flexibility. My next task was to learn how to predict the perfect day in order to be sure that a game fishing boat would be available during the busy marlin fishing season. The first day that I worked on this photograph I wasn't satisfied with the results so I chartered the boat again two weeks later.

Camera: Tomiyama, lens Nikkor SW90,   **Film:** Fuji 100ASA,   **Shutter speed:** 1/125 second,   **Filters:** polarizing,   **Cropping:** none,   **Time/Conditions:** mid-afternoon

Limited Edition release: 360 only worldwide,   **Exclusivity:** open

A unique view standing on a sand cay in the middle of the Great Barrier Reef, looking back towards the Australian coastline.

The Great Barrier Reef exhibits some spectacular islands out in the ocean; some are newly-formed islands like these sand cays on coral reefs. These sand cays are natural wonders that inspire awe in those who visit. Local boat owners sail out to these cays to spend the weekend in the clear night light under the stars. Visitors take trips on various vessels that visit the cays daily, or with helicopters or seaplanes that land right on the cays. One of the cays, Michaelmas Cay, is a sanctuary for a wide variety of sea birds that raise their young there.

Camera: Linhoff Technorama, Super Angulon 72 mm lens,   **Film:** Fuji Velvia 100F,   **Shutter speed:** 1/125 second,   **Filters:** polarized,   **Cropping:** none,   **Time/Conditions:** morning
Limited Edition release: 360 only worldwide,   **Exclusivity:** open

A sand cay in the Great Barrier Reef, Australia.

In the middle of shooting this scene I heard the sound of a light aircraft drawing closer and closer, until it landed right in the middle of my shot! It proceeded to turn around and park next to the sand cay.

Camera: Tomiyama, lens Nikkor SW90, **Film:** Fuji 100ASA, **Shutter speed:** 1/125 second, **Filters:** polarized, **Cropping:** none, **Time/Conditions:** mid-day

Limited Edition release: 360 only worldwide, **Exclusivity:** open

Michaelmas Cay, on the Great Barrier Reef, is a wonderful place to visit. The day that I visited, there would have been about 30,000 birds nesting there. Looking closely on the left it is possible to see some eggs. I also witnessed young chicks huddling beneath their mothers' wings. On this morning there was an easterly wind causing many of the birds to remain in flight. The sounds of the birds' squawking was almost deafening. This frame was the only one like it with a bird slowing to brake, its wings uplifted like an angel.

Camera: Linhoff Technorama, Super Angulon 72 mm lens,   **Film:** Fuji Velvia 100F,   **Shutter speed:** 1/125 second,   **Filters:** none,   **Cropping:** none,   **Time/Conditions:** windy, morning   **53**
Limited Edition release: 360 only worldwide,   **Exclusivity:** open

A sanctuary and breeding ground for a wide variety of sea birds. A popular destination to enjoy both the reef and bird life.

Camera: Linhoff Technorama, 180mm lens,   **Film:** Fuji Velvia 100F,   **Shutter speed:** 1/125 second,
Filters: polarized,   **Cropping:** none,   **Time/Conditions:** clear, mid-day
Limited Edition release: 360 only worldwide,   **Exclusivity:** open

Low Isles, a classic island on the Great Barrier Reef.

Camera: Tomiyama, lens Nikkor SW90,　**Film:** Fuji 100ASA,　**Shutter speed:** 1/125 second,
Filters: polarized,　**Cropping:** none,　**Time/Conditions:** early morning
Limited Edition release: 360 only worldwide,　**Exclusivity:** open

A typical rainforest creek flowing fresh and clear, Queensland Australia.
The World Heritage listed Daintree National Park rainforest is considered to be one of the oldest rainforest wilderness areas of the world. This richly dense rainforest goes right down to the coastal beaches. The high mountains are almost always covered by cloud, bringing fresh rain that retains the moisture in the rainforest and feeds the streams and rivers that flow through the area.

Camera: Linhoff Technorama, 180mm lens, **Film:** Fuji 100ASA, **Shutter speed:** 2 minutes, **Filters:** none, **Cropping:** none, **Time/Conditions:** cloudy, morning

Limited Edition release: 360 only worldwide, **Exclusivity:** open

At the base of Queensland's highest mountain, Mt. Bartle Frere 5,288 feet (1,612 meters), is Josephine Falls. Set amongst the rich rainforest of the tropics, these falls have beautiful, crystal-clear waters.

Camera: Tomiyama, lens Nikkor SW90,   **Film:** Fuji 100ASA,   **Shutter speed:** 1/4 seconds,   **Filters:** none,   **Cropping:** none,   **Time/Conditions:** 7am
Limited Edition release: 360 only worldwide,   **Exclusivity:** open

Millaa Millaa

Millaa Millaa Falls is one of the most photogenic, fairytale-like waterfalls in the world.
I had wanted to photograph the Millaa Millaa falls for a long time. Previously, there had been a period of more than two years that was completely dry; even the usually lush rainforests had been on fire. This photograph was taken toward the end of the following wet season. The scene appears almost unreal because it is just so perfect. There are various flowers and palms growing in view: Cordyline terminalas, White Perfume Ginger, and a Scaly Tree fern.

Camera: Linhoff Technorama, Super Angulon 72 mm lens, **Film:** Fuji 100ASA, **Shutter speed:** 2 minutes, **Filters:** none, **Cropping:** full frame, **Time/Conditions:** cloudy, morning
Limited Edition release: 360 only worldwide, **Exclusivity:** open

Mossman Queensland, Australia.

This river has an energy and life about it that is very special for me - the power of the water, the lighting, a glow behind the boulders, and a view that draws the eyes up to the Jurassic looking mountains in the distance. I arrived around 6am and within a short time, came to the area I wanted to photograph from. To my delight, I found that the lighting was just perfect, a soft, mauve light warming the whole river. I couldn't believe that everything could be so right on my first attempt, that is until I started to make my way to the middle of the river. It was swollen. The water was over my shoulders and fast flowing. There was no way I could get to my vantage point with all my camera gear over my shoulders. On that day, all I could do was watch.

Later I returned with a small rubber boat which I lugged up with all the camera gear to access the middle of the river and set up, hoping for the lighting. It took six attempts to capture this scene, but it was worth it.

Camera: Tomiyama, lens Nikkor SW90, **Film:** Fuji Velvia 100F, **Shutter speed:** 1/4 second, **Filters:** none, **Cropping:** none, **Time/Conditions:** early morning
Limited Edition release: 360 only worldwide, **Exclusivity:** open

Cairns, Australia.
A pond of pink lilies with a variety of colored leaves, shot with the early morning light casting long shadows.

Camera: Tomiyama, lens Nikkor SW90, **Film:** Fuji Velvia 100F, **Shutter speed:** 1/4 second, **Filters:** none, **Cropping:** full frame, **Time/Conditions:** early morning

Limited Edition release: 360 only worldwide, **Exclusivity:** open

Camera: Tomiyama, lens Nikkor SW90,   **Film:** Fuji 100ASA,   **Shutter speed:** 8 seconds,
Filters: none,   **Cropping:** none,   **Time/Conditions:** early morning
Limited Edition release: 360 only worldwide,   **Exclusivity:** open

"The Eternal Fig" has a wonderful angelic feel about it. With her branches reaching for the sky, ferns in her arms, warm sunlight and water still glistening from recent rains.

After many times hiking through this area, I was drawn to this magnificent tree by the roots that stretch like piping across the ground for 50 yards in every direction. The tree seems to have her arms out-stretched to heaven, the queen of the forest with ferns as her royal subjects.

"The Eternal Fig" is the very first frame after 40 minutes of rain. Sunlight glistens everywhere, the warm tones hum in the brightness. The sky has a fantastic heavenly radiance due to the long exposure. Previous frames were exposed as long as 9 minutes - too long. And frames taken afterwards were marred by droplets on the lens that refused to dry.

It was a long time before I was brave enough to bring all my camera gear into the rain, but it was worth it. This was the seventh attempt to photograph this tree in three weeks of trying.

Camera: Tomiyama, lens Nikkor SW90, **Film:** Fuji 100ASA, **Shutter speed:** 2 minutes, **Filters:** none,
Cropping: none, **Time/Conditions:** 7am, just after light rain
Limited Edition release: 360 only worldwide, **Exclusivity:** open

Port Douglas, Australia.

Very few pictures in my collection were taken spontaneously and without any planning. Tropical Vibrance is one of them.

I was in the process of working on several concepts for the area, this particular occasion on the palm trees that line the northern end of this beach. I arrived at the beach early. While I was getting ready for the sunrise I was overwhelmed by the color and the cloud formations. Needless to say, I left the palm trees and shot this scene. There were, however, a lot of mosquitoes. I literally shot only three frames before being totally swarmed by them. They even chased me back to the car! From that day, insect repellent became an essential item in my kit.

Camera: Tomiyama, lens Nikkor SW90,　**Film:** Fuji Velvia 50ASA,　**Shutter speed:** 20 seconds,　**Filters:** None,　**Cropping:** none,　**Time/Conditions:** sunrise
Limited Edition release: 360 only worldwide,　**Exclusivity:** open

70   Palm Cove

Palm Cove, Australia.
I worked on this scene over a number of weeks. I love the perspective of the waves leading off to the distance. Looking closely, it is possible to see subtle ripples in the sand under the water in the forward centre of the frame.

Camera: Tomiyama, lens Nikkor SW90,   **Film:** Fuji 100ASA,   **Shutter speed:** 1/15 second,   **Filters:** None,   **Cropping:** none,   **Time/Conditions:** sunrise
Limited Edition release: 160 only worldwide,   **Exclusivity:** open

Palm Cove Sunrise

Camera: Tomiyama, lens Nikkor SW90, **Film:** Fuji Velvia 100ASA, **Shutter speed:** 15 seconds, **Filters:** none, **Cropping:** none, **Time/Conditions:** sunrise
Limited Edition release: 160 only worldwide, **Exclusivity:** open

Cairns, Australia.
Perfectly blue sky, perfectly calm waters, a perfectly still day - altogether a beautiful day in the tropics.

Camera: Tomiyama, lens SW90,　**Film:** Fuji 100ASA,　**Shutter speed:** 1/125 second,
Filters: Polarized,　**Cropping:** none,　**Time/Conditions:** midday
Limited Edition release: 360 only worldwide,　**Exclusivity:** open

Port Douglas, Australia.
Captured in the early morning light, Four Mile Beach glows in the warmth of sunrise. This location offers a popular morning walk down to the end of the beach with the headland in the distance.

Camera: Linhoff Technorama, Super Angulon 72 mm lens, **Film:** Fuji 100 ASA, **Filters:** none,
Cropping: none, **Shutter speed:** 1/30 second, **Time/Conditions:** just after sunrise
Limited Edition release: 160 only worldwide, **Exclusivity:** open

Capturing this frame was very challenging. It's an instant exposure that took eight days to achieve. The difficulty with lightning is that it is only there for the briefest time. The phrase "Can we try that again?" is not applicable - once it flashes, it's gone. To capture this type of photograph you need to storm chase; in this case I chased storms for eight days with the intention of returning in a couple of weeks. Every night for eight days I had no sleep. My eyes were fixed on the heavens, watching for storms that might come my way. Higher Power was shot at 5am on the seventh morning. It was a strange storm traveling in the opposite direction of all the previous storms. It all came together so beautifully. A long, narrow stretch of cloud filled the frame perfectly. The cloud dissipated above me so that no rain and no lightning would fall on me. The moon was sitting behind the cloud adding to the magnificent mauve tone that illuminates this image. Originally I wanted to name this photograph 'Angel's Wings', inspired by the faint glow behind the lighting that looks like an angel.

This was a very powerful twin strike. A few days before, in the same spot, lightning was striking all around me - scary!

Camera: Tomiyama, lens Nikkor SW90, **Film:** Fuji 100ASA, **Shutter speed:** 3 minutes, **Filters:** none, **Cropping:** 5%, **Time/Conditions:** 5am
Limited Edition release: 360 only worldwide, **Exclusivity:** open

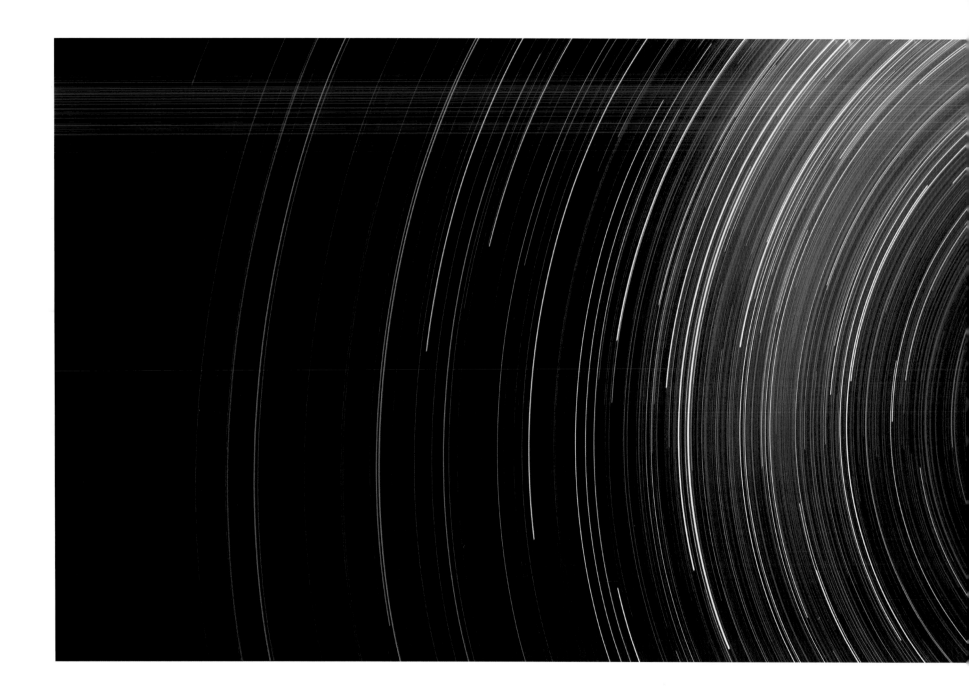

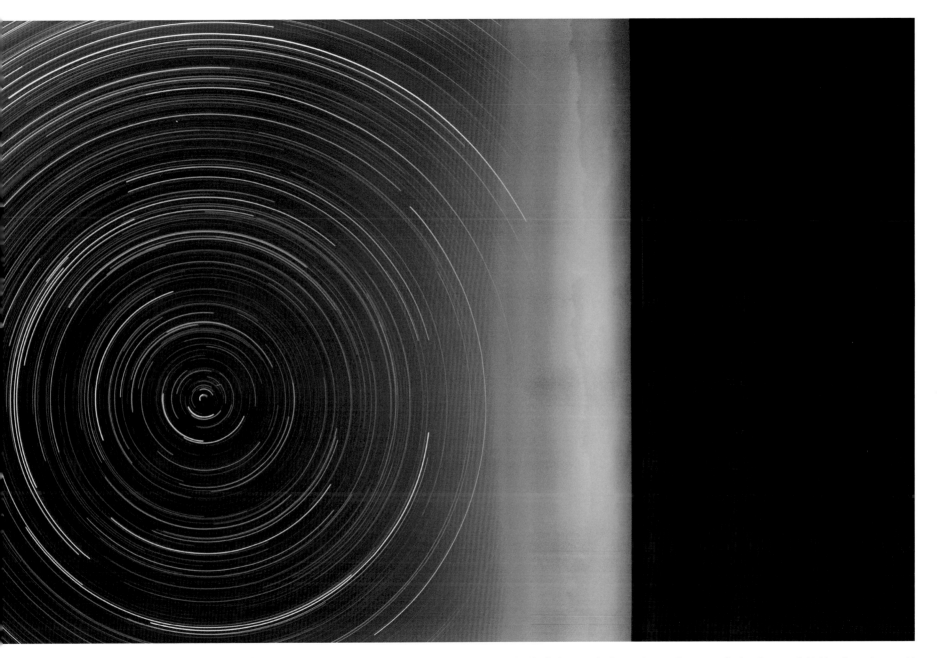

This image began as an idea one night whilst camping under the stars. The original idea was to capture stars through the clouds that I saw in the morning. As the concept developed, I started thinking about what I could 'squeeze' into the frame. There are essentially three parts to this image: the "Southern Cross", the South Celestial Pole and the dusk light. The photograph was captured over five months, needing remote, clear, cloudless, pollution free, light free locations; and without the moon. Typically there are only several days a month to try to capture the stars in this way so that the moon does not interfere with the shot.

The shot itself was a six and a half hour exposure pointing the camera due south with the bottom of the frame touching the horizon and the top of the frame right up to the top of the sky. The brightest stars are both the Southern Cross constellation and the "Pointers". The South Celestial Pole is in the centre of the circles.

An additional technical challenge was the re-shooting, on the same film, of a sunset over the ocean (double exposure).

Camera: Tomiyama, lens Nikkor SW90,   **Film:** Kodak 100ASA,   **Shutter speed:** 6 hours 24 minutes,   **Filters:** none,   **Cropping:** none,   **Time/Conditions:** clear
Limited Edition release: 360 only worldwide,   **Exclusivity:** open

Uluṟu-Kata Tjuṯa National Park – World Heritage Area, Central Australia.
The rich red glow on the horizon, red and yellow dusk with the black of the night sky and in the presence of Kata Tjuṯa (Olgas).

Camera: Tomiyama, lens Nikkor SW90,   **Film:** Fuji Velvia 50ASA,   **Shutter speed:** 20 seconds,   **Filters:** none,   **Time/Conditions:** 45 minutes after sunset
Limited Edition release: 360 only worldwide,   **Exclusivity:** open

Simpson Desert, Central Australia.
The brilliant, rich red of the Simpson Desert at dawn, with the soft, early morning light gently touching over the landscape. The evidence that a lizard and a dingo have passed by is their footsteps, left in the sand.

Camera: Tomiyama, lens Nikkor SW90,   **Film:** Fuji 100ASA,   **Shutter speed:** 1/2 second,   **Filters:** none,   **Cropping:** none,   **Time/Conditions:** sunset
Limited Edition release: 360 only worldwide,   **Exclusivity:** open

Spacious

Spending a length of time in desert areas is an immense experience. The absence of anything, except space and blue sky, is astounding. I particularly liked the different shades of color: the deep sky blue sky blending into the yellow-pink hue before touching the horizon. I really wanted to capture all of this but felt there needed to be something to connect with … I found this hut in the middle of nowhere. This photograph was captured just at sunrise, with the light casting an infinitely long shadow.

Camera: Tomiyama, lens Nikkor SW90,   **Film:** Fuji Velvia 50ASA,   **Shutter speed:** 1 second,   **Filters:** None,   **Cropping:** none,   **Time/Conditions:** on sunrise

Limited Edition release: 360 only worldwide,   **Exclusivity:** open

Violet Ayers

Uluru-Kata Tjuṯa National Park - World Heritage Area, Central Australia.
Australia's great natural symbol, Ayers Rock (Uluru), is a giant, monolithic rock standing alone in the vast deserts of Central Australia. Captured in a brilliant winter light, the richness of the reds are shown to their fullest extent. I spent almost a week photographing Ayers Rock and the Olgas. Of all the days I was there, I was very fortunate the day I photographed 'Violet Ayers'. Although it is a most inspiring location, no photograph can truly capture the grandeur of the area compared with seeing it in real life.

Camera: Tomiyama, lens Nikkor SW90, **Film:** Fuji 100ASA, **Shutter speed:** 2 minutes, **Filters:** none, **Cropping:** none, **Time/Conditions:** 20 minutes after sunset
Limited Edition release: 360 only worldwide, **Exclusivity:** open

The unbelievably red sand is almost orange. The sand's smoothness is the bed of small desert plants, their colors in contrast to the red. This scene shows Ayers Rock gradually rising in the distance with the silhouette of the Olgas on the right. Traveling around Ayers Rock is a wonderful experience. I could keep coming back again and again; I find that there is always something new to appreciate.

I searched the sand dunes for a vantage point of Ayers Rock and the Olgas that also had the pure red sand and some interesting plants, and I found a spot. During my first attempt I realized a problem: my shadow. I continued to search and found another place but this time with a bush that I could hide my shadow behind. The next morning I arrived back in the dark, I started to look for my spot again, being very careful not to walk on any areas of open clear sand. The trouble was that I couldn't find my spot and as the sky was brightening, I became a little anxious and accidentally walked right through the middle of my scene. At first I was disappointed, but on second thought, I now had a good name: "Walk About".

Camera: Tomiyama, lens Nikkor SW90, **Film:** Fuji 100ASA, **Shutter speed:** 4 seconds, **Filters:** none, **Cropping:** none, **Time/Conditions:** sunrise   89
Limited Edition release: 360 only worldwide, **Exclusivity:** open   Uluṟu-Kata Tjuṯa National Park - World Heritage Area, Central Australia

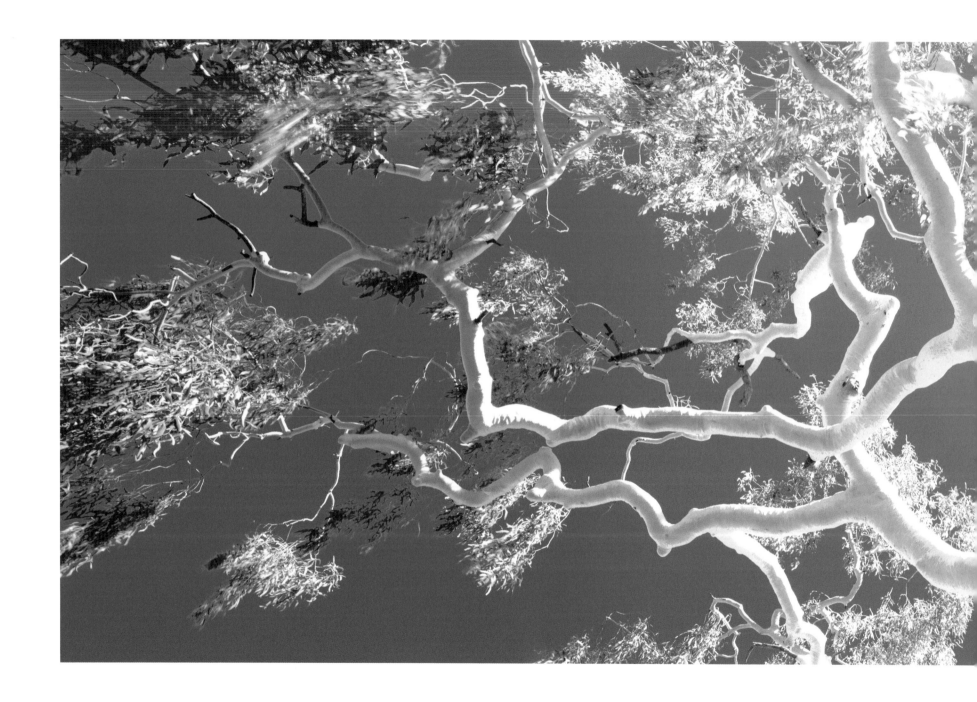

The desert of Central Australia has some of the most extraordinary deep blue skies and ghost gums with the purest and smoothest white skin. I had an idea about photographing white ghost gums with a dry red river bed ideally meandering off into the distance. I searched for my vision, looking in areas where it would be likely that I could find such a scene. I had driven on over 600 miles (1000km) of dirt road. As I was driving on this particular day, I came across this wonderful example of a ghost gum, but without the dry river bed. I couldn't help but hop out of the car and take a closer look. What a magnificent tree, and what wonderful white smooth curves and lines. I was struck by the contrast between the glow of the white against the dark blue sky.

I lay on my back with my head in the red sand, trying to get as much of the tree in the frame as possible. I squeezed under my camera with it pressing against my face. The one tree looked like two trees or was it that the two looked like one as their arms flowed together like hands waving in the air… "We Are One".

Camera: Tomiyama, lens Nikkor SW90, **Film:** Fuji 100ASA, **Shutter speed:** 1 second, **Filters:** none, **Cropping:** none, **Time/Conditions:** late morning
Limited Edition release: 360 only worldwide, **Exclusivity:** open

Kosciusko Spring

Australian alpine during spring, at the start of the Thredbo river.

I had spent the night in a tent at a lookout with a view over the fabulous Australian Alps (including Mt. Kosciusko). Arriving in the middle of the night, I quickly set up the tent, escaping the massive cloud of mosquitoes that happened to be there. In the morning after a good sleep, I awoke to a great view.

Down the road a ways, I came across this scene, a picture-perfect arrangement of a snow gum, alpine flora and a pristine alpine creek.

Camera: Tomiyama, lens Nikkor SW90, **Film:** Fuji Velvia 50ASA, **Shutter speed:** 20 seconds, **Filters:** none, **Time/Conditions:** sunrise, partially cloudy

Limited Edition release: 360 only worldwide, **Exclusivity:** open

Craig's Hut

A homestead in the mountains of Victoria, "Man from Snowy River", Victoria Australia. The Victorian mountains do amazing things for the soul; it's a wonder that all Victorians don't own horses. I camped here for six days, every morning and every evening getting up and waiting for some special lighting. I loved every minute of it - the freshness of the air, the sounds of the birds and forest, the snow gums, the peacefulness, the mountains and the beautiful views.

Through the hours and days that I was there, I shifted the camera many times because something wasn't right with the composition. On the last day, I got it right. It had started to rain heavily to my left, but the sky cleared to the right and then the sun rose and broke through the clouds, just enough to lighten up the edge of the rain, the posts, the rocks and the house - not too strong and not too dark - a perfect balance.

This hut was destroyed by bushfire in December 2006.

Camera: Tomiyama, lens Nikkor SW90,   **Film:** Fuji Velvia 50ASA,   **Shutter speed:** 2 minutes,   **Filters:** none,   **Cropping:** none,   **Time/Conditions:** on sunrise
Limited Edition release: 360 only worldwide,   **Exclusivity:** open

Alpine country, Australia.

"The branches turn, guided by Nature's love. The mist rolls in, connecting the lovers. Thus on a single branch, the droplet is formed. A balance of what is new, and what will be." (Poem by Paula Wilson.)

Two hours before this photograph was taken, large hail stones rained down on me for over half an hour, leaving me to cross flooded mountain rivers and streams, as low as 35°F (2°C) in temperature. The whole landscape was awash. I had been looking for snow gums for some time, making a number of trips into the mountains. Fortunately, I stumbled across these whilst trying to photograph some lakes on the opposite mountain range. A short time after discovery, because of the hail, fog swept up the valley and over the ridge where the snow gums were, making the conditions perfect.

Camera: Tomiyama, lens Nikkor SW90, **Film:** Fuji Velvia 50ASA, **Shutter speed:** 2 minutes, **Filters:** none, **Time/Conditions:** sunset / fog

Limited Edition release: 360 only worldwide, **Exclusivity:** open

Australia's beaches invite an appreciation for the clear air, an endless love for the ocean and the peacefulness of first light.

When I was young I spent every holiday at this beach; it is a very special place for me. I camped here for five days, several hundred yards away from this scene. Every morning I rose before sunrise in the hope of discovering special lighting. For the four days, each day was clear and sunny - nothing exciting. On the fifth day, however, there was some cloud and haze on the horizon to soften the sun, and a line of cloud to pick up the light. Perfect! (Named after Johann Sebastian Bach's "Air On The G String".)

Camera: Tomiyama, lens Nikkor SW90,   **Film:** Fuji Velvia 50ASA,   **Shutter speed:** 1 second,   **Filters:** none,   **Cropping:** none,   **Time/Conditions:** on sunrise
Limited Edition release: 360 only worldwide,   **Exclusivity:** open

NSW, Australia.

This area of Australia is very special, featuring wild kangaroos & parrots that are tame enough to feed and handle. There are also secluded beaches; some of sand, some of smooth colored rocks, and others of shells and coral. I photographed this scene over a few months, trying to balance the high tide (which was needed for the waterfalls) with a soft clouded sunrise. To be sure I had captured what I wanted, I returned to photograph the scene again. With perfect conditions, I set up with great anticipation, only to have a freak wave crash up and soaked all of my camera gear with hundreds of gallons of salt water!

Camera: Tomiyama, lens Nikkor SW90,   **Film:** Fuji Velvia 50ASA,   **Shutter speed:** 4 seconds,   **Filters:** none,   **Cropping:** none,   **Time/Conditions:** sunrise
Limited Edition release: 360 only worldwide,   **Exclusivity:** open

Victoria, Australia.

Someone once said, 'Lighthouses are a monument to the determination of man.' Although I had researched lighthouse locations over a few months, this lighthouse was discovered by accident. It turned out to be the first sighting of Australia by Captain Cook of the Endeavour, named Hicks Point, after the first mate.

I returned to this location on two or three occasions, driving 500 miles (800km) return each time, attempting to capture this classically beautiful scene. From the campsite it was a two hour return hike. I made the hike a dozen times before this amazing color came. The sky turned this brilliant pink. The waves crashed over the rocks and a storm cloud moved in on the right; it was a very powerful experience. Occasionally when there are very high clouds and the sun is setting, for a very short time the clouds turn a brilliant pink.

Camera: Tomiyama, lens Nikkor SW90,   **Film:** Fuji Velvia 50ASA,   **Shutter speed:** 2 minutes,   **Filters:** none,   **Cropping:** none,   **Time/Conditions:** 15 minutes past sunset

Limited Edition release: 360 only worldwide,   **Exclusivity:** open

Victoria, Australia.

The great coastline of Australia burns hot red as it meets the vast, unhindered Southern Ocean. The Great Ocean Road is along a fantastic stretch of coastline and the name of the road expresses the wonder. Situated west of Melbourne, the road travels through lush green farmland with rolling hills, sandstone cliffs, rugged coastline and windswept land further to the west.

In southern Australia, Spring can bring changeable weather. I camped here for a number of days waiting for the sun to come out. Deciding not to wait any longer, I traveled inland and further explored Victoria. About a week later, in the middle of the afternoon, I noticed a change in the weather. As I was only 120 miles (200km) away from the 12 Apostles, I made a dash for the sunset, hoping to have a bit of clear sky on the horizon. When I arrived, the cloud had started to cover the sky again but just before the horizon it shone out in all it's glory.

Camera: Tomiyama, lens Nikkor SW90,   **Film:** Fuji Velvia 50ASA,   **Shutter speed:** 8 seconds,   **Filters:** None,   **Cropping:** none,   **Time/Conditions:** sunset

Limited Edition release: 360 only worldwide,   **Exclusivity:** open

A pristine mountain creek, central Japan

Traveling in Japan in the mountain regions, there are so many beautiful rivers and creeks. Japan has an abundant supply of water. In the country areas especially, you can always hear the sound of flowing water. The name of the village that is near here can be literally translated as "Naturally Air Conditioned Village", after the cold air that flows out of the caves. They even use some of this air to cool the office buildings. This creek is freezing cold, hence the jade colored water.

Camera: Tomiyama, lens Nikkor SW90,   **Film:** Fuji 100ASA,   **Shutter speed:** 4 seconds,   **Filters:** none,   **Cropping:** none,   **Time/Conditions:** morning
Limited Edition release: 750 only worldwide,   **Exclusivity:** open

A cold water mountain swimming hole, central Japan

Set in a steep valley, this creek starts its travels high in the hills. Following it down I came across this calm pool; it was cold but what a picture-perfect scene. I set up my tripod and camera with the water waist high and shot this scene. Places like this make all the exploring and traveling that I do worthwhile, when I come across these scenes tucked away in their perfect setting.

Camera: Tomiyama, lens Nikkor SW90, **Film:** Fuji 100ASA, **Shutter speed:** 2 minutes, **Filters:** none, **Cropping:** none, **Time/Conditions:** morning
Limited Edition release: 750 only worldwide, **Exclusivity:** open

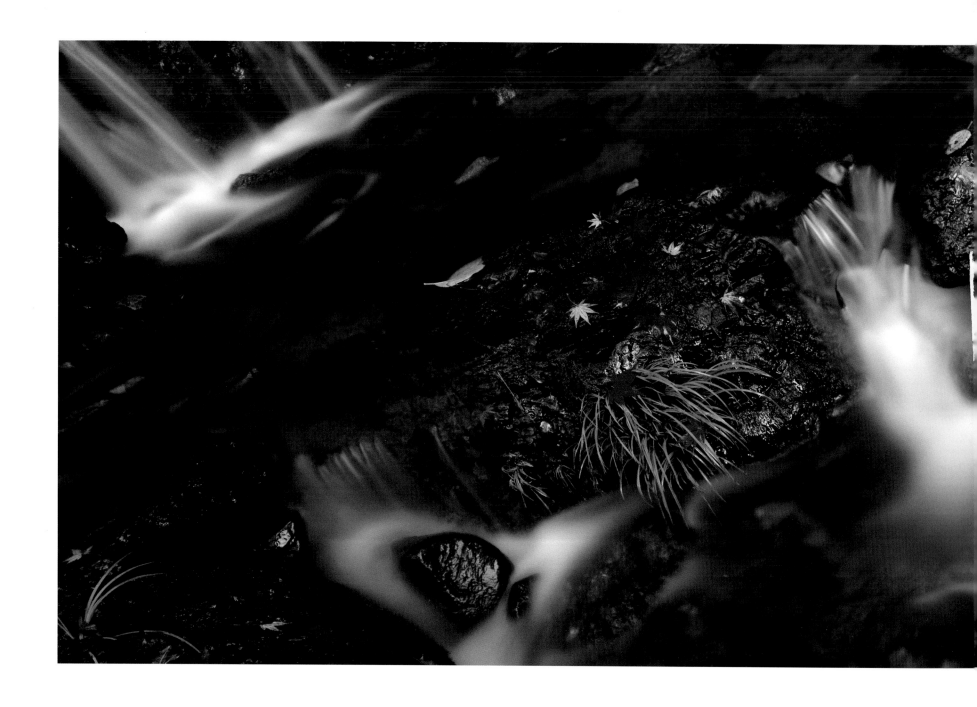

There is a tranquility in the abundance of natural streams; this scene was found just outside the grounds of a beautiful temple in the mountains of Gifu, Japan.

Traveling around the maze of small mountain roads, I came to the end of one to find a small town with a temple with high walls. It had its own forest of maple trees, with a traditional red bridge over the stream. I returned to the town at the peak of the Fall reds and oranges, and when patchy cloud was expected: blue sky to bring out the water colors and cloud for color balance. I splashed water on the rocks, on the greenery and leaves to help bring out the colors and captured this scene.

Later I returned and photographed the scene again to make sure that I had achieved the photograph that I wanted. The first set of photographs was best, but I returned a third time, just to be sure - but the river was covered by piles of yellow, dry, old maple leaves a foot thick.

Camera: Tomiyama, lens Nikkor SW90,   **Film:** Fuji Velvia 50ASA,   **Shutter speed:** 2 minutes,   **Filters:** none,   **Cropping:** none,   **Time/Conditions:** mid-morning   **111**
Limited Edition release: 750 only worldwide,   **Exclusivity:** open

In the deserts of Australia, the pink glow on the horizon always rises as the sun goes down.

This land is so isolated! Pictured is a road with no through traffic; no-one on the way to anywhere. The road that I was on eventually connects with a road that lead to Australia's biggest lake, Lake Eyre, 230 feet (70 meters) below sea level and bone dry. I carried food for 10 days, with 100 liters of spare water and fuel to drive 900 miles (1,500 km). In two days I did not pass a single car. The weather was not hot at all, compared with the 100°F (38°C) that it reached only a few weeks before. Summer had almost arrived, but it waited for me.

Camera: Tomiyama, lens SW90,   **Film:** Fuji 100ASA,   **Shutter speed:** 1 second,
Filters: none,   **Cropping:** none,   **Time/Conditions:** sunset
Limited Edition release: 360 only worldwide,   **Exclusivity:** open

ABOUT THE ARTIST

Ric Steininger's passion for photography emerged at a young age. With the combination of a sense of adventure and his appreciation for light, photography appealed greatly to him. Ric was inspired to shoot the grandeur of the natural world, traveling extensively for the sole reason of capturing something unique – something "painted by Nature". Ric worked as a freelance photographer in his home city of Canberra, Australia with great success. But Ric never forgot his first love, and not being satisfied he set off with a panoramic camera to shoot 'art' on this grand format. In 1991, Ric started using a 6x17cm film (2¼ x 7") panoramic camera, a simple camera with a single lens; it has no battery, and no light meter. It is far from the digital automated cameras that other photographers use today. It takes masterful technical skill to successfully operate the camera in the many and varied environments photographed.

Ric is a self-taught photographer who started with a developing vision and a small book on photographic technique. He treated his earlier expeditions like an university degree, studying the natural world in relation to capturing it on film. Ric spent five years shooting with the panoramic camera before he held his first exhibition in January 1997 at the Sheraton Mirage, Port Douglas, Australia. The exhibitions that followed were met with great success and by May 1997, Ric opened up his first gallery in Cairns, Australia.

Ric has always operated a little unconventionally, going to great lengths to capture a single frame. Ric generally sets out with a clear vision of what he is looking for. It starts with an idea, sometimes sketched on paper. Then he sets out in search of it, researching locations and potential sites. Ric can be off for weeks until he finds the perfect scene and viewpoint that would fit into the lens of his camera with drama and life. The actual shooting – the firing of the shutter – might only take a second or so, but it may have taken a week or more for all the conditions to be just right. Lighting is an unpredictable thing, and along with all the anomalies like wind, cloud and seasons, it can be difficult to get all the variables right at the one time. In addition to the creative processes on site, the journey to the site itself often requires long hikes and climbs, dangerous cliff lines, mountains, and even lava crossings. But to Ric, it's all worth it when the final shot is captured.

Ric loves natural light, and the various ways that it can play across a scene. Ric never uses color filters – ever – but chooses to work with what is presented to him; he is a purist in terms of the use of natural light. To him photography is somewhat like sailing; Ric loves being out in the elements, with the wind in his face and set on a specific direction and purpose. He enjoys the challenge of navigating through and working with the conditions. Sometimes a stormy night clears; the morning brings a calm and brilliant light sets the scene aglow. All of the elements have come together and the shutter is fired.

This collection is being released as Ric celebrates the opening of the newest Ric Steininger Galleries in Lahaina, Hawaii and Las Vegas.